Learn French through music!

The SUBLingual "Listen. Read. Listen. Learn" method
helps to motivate, inspire and encourage learning
a new language thru music and lyrics.
This book is designed to help you pick up words
and phrases in conjunction with standard courses
and traditional learning methods.

Published by Sublingual Music Group
Los Angeles, CA
www.sublingualmusic.com

Distributed by Greenleaf Book Group
For ordering information or special discounts for bulk purchases,
please contact Greenleaf Book Group LLC
PO Box 91869, Austin, TX 78709
512.891.6100

Design composition by Andrea Young at Anomaly Ad Group
SUBLingual French updated by Kate Wojtan at magicmustache.com
Music licensed by SUBLingual Music. See credits page for more information

Publisher's Cataloging-In-Publication Data
(Prepared by The Donohue Group, Inc.)

Smith, Kyla.
Learn French through music! / [by Kyla Smith]. -- 1st ed.

p. : col.ill. ; cm. + 1 sound disc.

Text in English; song lyrics in French and English.
ISBN: 978-0-9801427-2-3

1. French language--Conversation and phrase books--English. 2. French language--Sound recordings for English speakers. 3. French language--Self-instruction. 4. French language--Study and teaching--Audio-visual aids. 5. Songs, French. I. Title.

PC2121 .S65 2010
448.3421 2010924633

Part of the Tree Neutral™ program, which offsets the number of trees consumed in the production and printing of this book by taking proactive steps, such as planting trees in direct proportion to the number of trees used: www.treeneutral.com.
Printed in China on acid-free paper.

10 11 12 13 14 15 10 9 8 7 6 5 4 3 2 1

First Edition

Table of Contents

French Speaking Countries

Belgium
Benin
Burkina Faso
Burundi
Cameroon
Canada .
Central African Republic
Chad
Comoros
Côte d`Lvoire
Democratic Republic of Congo
Djibouti
Equatorial Guinea
France
Gabon
Guinea
Haiti
Luxembourg
Madagascar
Mali
Monaco
Niger
Rwanda
Senegal
Seychelles
Switzerland
Togo
Vanuatu

Inspire language.
Inspire travel.
Inspire music...

That is our mission.
www.sublingual.com

France

France

Northern

Southern

France

Best time to visit April–June OR Sept.–Nov.

Northern

MUST SEE:

1. Loire Valley – drive from Blois to Saumur… one of the most relaxing yet breathtaking drives in the world. As a buffer between the North and Southern France, it has remained a stronghold of French Royalty for generations. Thus, providing a cross-sectional of 1000 years French architectural history.
2. Normandy – visit where D-Day got its name from WWII at Normandy's Utah and Omaha's Beaches. Pay a visit to Rouen – historic city housing the famous Gothic cathedral depicted perfectly in Monet's famous "Rouen Cathedral".
3. Brittney – Adopting its own unique set of food and culture, Brittney or "Brenton's" as they are called have developed a pseudo country within a country. Less populated then most of southern France by comparison; Brittney's rich & mysterious interior is a great place for hiking, river rafting or exploring by boat.

GEOGRAPHY:
Lush green forests, picturesque vineyards lay inland while white sandy beaches run up along the north.

SAY:
C'est la vie! "that's life" or "such is life"

Flemish-inspired food. Try **'flamiche'** which means cake. Made with anything from leeks to strong cheese.

Southern

GEOGRAPHY:
French Alps in the east, rolling hills and lush green landscapes inland and ocean views of the Mediterranean along the south.

SAY:
Crème de lá Crème
"Best of the Best"

EAT:
Ratatouille

MUST-DO'S:

1. French Alps – Offers a wide range of activities ranging from skiing to cannoning, the French Alps are a heritage to European vacation spots. Check out the Parc National de la Vanoise south of Tignes – amazing waterfalls, canyons and wildlife.
2. French Riviera – Monaco, Nice, Cannes and St Tropez are a few names that everyone has heard of for a good reason. Beautiful idyllic settings along the Mediterranean.
3. Corsica – While the enchanted island of Corsica has an ever-ending love/ hate relationship with the mainland, it still proves to be one of the top highlights of visiting France. Depending on where you depart, the island is a mere 3-5 hour ferry ride from France and well worth the wait.

France

Paris

Paris

Best time to visit April–June OR Sept.–Nov.

With more famous landmarks than any other place in the world, Paris has locked in the #1 travel destination spot in the world. With all of the sight-seeing to be had, make sure to soak up the culture by strolling along the cobblestone alleys, sipping coffee for hours at a café while enjoying the relaxed Parisian lifestyle.

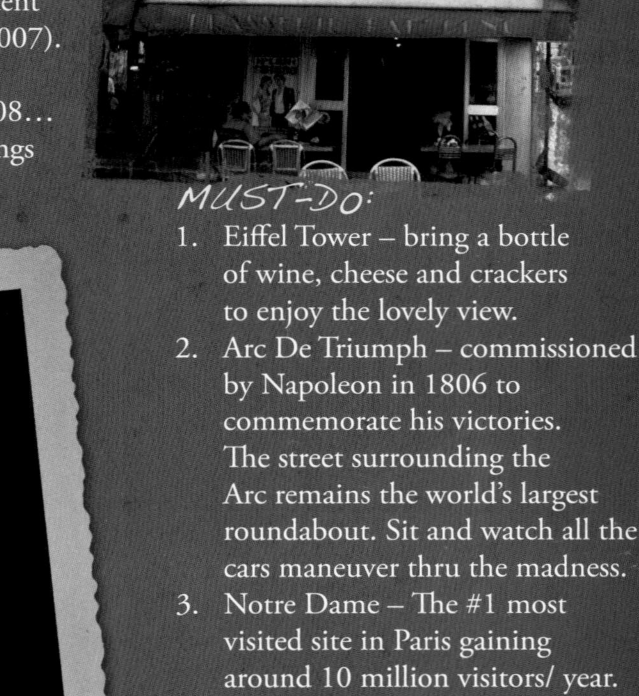

FUN FACT:

Nicolas Sarkozy is the current President of France (won by popular vote in 2007). He is also married to world famous model and singer Carla Bruni in 2008… if you haven't noticed; two of her songs are on this album)!

MUST-DO:

1. Eiffel Tower – bring a bottle of wine, cheese and crackers to enjoy the lovely view.
2. Arc De Triumph – commissioned by Napoleon in 1806 to commemorate his victories. The street surrounding the Arc remains the world's largest roundabout. Sit and watch all the cars maneuver thru the madness.
3. Notre Dame – The #1 most visited site in Paris gaining around 10 million visitors/ year. The cathedral is a masterpiece of French Gothic architecture. A bronze star set from the pavement across from the main entrance marks the exact location of "point zero" of all French roads.
4. Museums – Louvre & Musee d'Orsay are two of the most famous museums in the world housing world-famous masterpieces.

EAT:

Crepes-hundreds of combinations

SAY:

"Joie de vivre" (high on life)

ECONOMY/GOVERNMENT:

Paris today is one of the world's leading hubs for business and cultural attractions. Forty-five million tourists visit Paris every year, thus leading tourism to be a main source of the economy.

Canada

Canada

Canada

Quebec is the only province in Canada whose primary language is French. There are about 5 million French Canadians living in the province, and most all have come from descendants of French explorers and colonists that came over hundreds of years ago.

NOTE:

The French spoken in Canada is essentially the same as what you'd hear in France. However, there are some differences - just as there are between English in Australia, and English in New Zealand. The local tongue is known as 'Quebecois'. As with most countries, any attempt to speak the local language is much appreciated.

SAY:

"Tout le kit"- the whole shebang, the whole kit and caboodle… everything.

EAT:

Poutine- [poo teen] is a scrumptious creation of french fries, gravy and melted cheese curds that's as unhealthy as it is delicious.

MUST-DO'S:

1. Quebec City – As one of the few remaining walled cities in the world, it's pristine and charm has been manifested as one of the most charming cities. Quebec is made up of what's called "Old Upper Town" and an "Old Lower Town". To get immersed in the culture, just sit down at one of the hundreds of corner cafes to hang out and talk to the locals.
2. Niagara Falls – There are really no words to describe this awe-inspiring natural attraction. Even though Niagara ranks 50th of 'tall' waterfalls, the shear amount of water that falls here brings 14 million visitors annually. Fun-fact: A million bathtubs of water plummet over the edge every second.
3. Montreal – With an all-inclusive European vibe, Montreal has some of the best nightlife Canada has to offer. Also know for their completeness of menu options, Montreal is the "Pangaea" of food. From authentic phó noodles shops to piles of Italian spaghetti.

ECONOMY/GOVERNMENT:

The government is a constitutional monarchy. This form of government has the vote for the most peaceful system. Other adopters are: Australia, Belgium, Denmark, Sweden, Thailand, Netherlands and the UK.

GEOGRAPHY:

- Capital: Ottawa
- Population: 33.8 Million

France

Monaco

Monaco

Monaco

Monaco is the second-largest city-state in the world (following the Vatican City in Rome). As one of the smallest countries in the world, its main attraction is the Hotel & Casino Monte Carlo.
Previous to it being built in 1865, Monaco was one of the world's poorest states. Following the completion of the Monte Carlo spawned a dramatic surge in the economy; bringing world class restaurants, gambling and over-the-top luxurious lodgings for the rich and famous.

GEOGRAPHY:

- As a city-state only measuring only 2km, it takes a visitor roughly 56 minutes to walk the width of the country.
- Capital: Monte Carlo
- Population: 33,000

ECONOMY:

Primarily tourism & gambling (even though citizens of Monaco are not allowed to enter the gambling quarters).

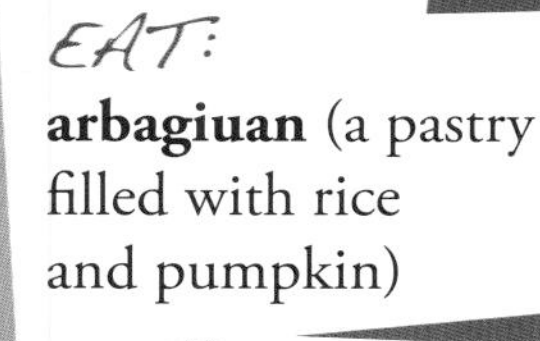

EAT:
arbagiuan (a pastry filled with rice and pumpkin)

SAY:

Crème de la crème- "the best of the best"

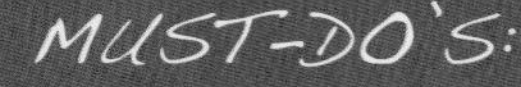

1. Place a bet James Bond style at the Hotel Monte Carlo
2. Formula 1 Grand Prix – annually held in Monaco and sets the stage for the worlds rich and famous to visit.
3. Dream big – take a walk along the harbor and see the incredible yachts that can have a pretty price tag of up to hundreds of millions!

Switzerland

Switzerland

Switzerland

Switzerland is one of the richest countries in the world with a nominal per capita GDP of $67,384. Two primary cities in Switzerland – Zürich and Geneva have respectively been ranked as having the second and third highest quality of life in the world.

Because Switzerland sits as a land-locked country in Europe, it also claims Italian, German and Romansh as its official languages. Due to it's hodgepodge of descendants, the Swiss do not form a nation in the sense of a common ethnic or linguistic identity, but primarily from historical background and shared values.

ECONOMY:

Switzerland has been the wealthiest countries in Europe for most of the last 100 years. Home to many large multi-national companies in various sectors such as health, pharmaceutical, measuring, machinery and watches

SAY:

Grüezi (German)
Bonjour (French)
Buongiorno (Italian)

EAT:

Dairy products: Chocolate, Cheese or anything **fondue** style!

MUST-DO'S:

1. Zurich – Most populous city, financial hub and home to best nightlife the Swiss have to offer. Named as the city with the best quality of life, a lot can be learned from hanging out with the locals.
2. Interlaken – Mecca for adventure-seeking backpackers offering skydiving, cannoning, hang gliding, paragliding and skiing. Take a trip up to Gimmelwald which is a small town that can only be accessed thru the Schilthorn gondola made famous by the James Bond flick.
3. Lucerne – Medieval town offering many historical landmarks. Also an essential stop while passing along the Alps.

Best time to visit May–Sept.

GEOGRAPHY:

- Swiss Alps to the south – one of best skiing spots in the world
- Most of the population abides in the plateau in the "middleland" which is mostly beautiful hilly green countryside
- Capital: Bern
- Population: 7.6 Million

Africa

Africa

Cote d'Ivoire

Cameroon

Africa

Many countries in Africa claim French as their national language, though many have a native local tongue. The following is info on the largest populations in Africa where French is commonly spoken.

Cameroon

Best time to visit Nov.-Feb.

Some call this country "miniature Africa' for its geological and cultural diversity. Everything you would want to experience in Africa, Cameroon has to offer including beaches, deserts, mountains, rainforests, and savannas. Though it sits in a tough neighborhood, bordered by some problematic countries, its is commonly visited by tourists.

GEOGRAPHY:

- Capital: Yaoundé
- Population: 20 Million

TO-DO:

1. Mt Cameroon – highest peak in West Africa and a still-active volcano.
2. Parc National de Waza – one of the best National Parks in the region with abundant wildlife including elephants and unique indigenous creatures.
3. Kribi – hang out on the white sandy beaches and practice your French with the locals over freshly-caught grilled seafood.

Cote d'Lvoire

Best time to visit Nov.-Feb.

Cote d'lvoire (often referred to as the "Ivory Coast") was once praised as one of Africa's economic miracles until about 2002 when a northern-led rebellion that violently split the country in half. Since then, most of the French citizens have jumped ship and the economy has since fallen apart. The country still has some of the most pure natural resources in West Africa – such as the National Park containing a vast patch of untapped rainforest and a string of breathtaking beaches along the Atlantic coast.

GEOGRAPHY:

- Capital: Yamoussoukro
- Population: 21 Million

TO-DO:

1. Yamoussoukro – check out the Basilique de Notre Dame de la Paix – a perfect replica of Rome's St. Peter's Basilica.
2. Parc National de Tai – one of the largest remaining areas of virgin rainforests in West Africa.
3. Man – known as the "city of 18 mountains" is well use to visitors and all villages are accessible by car or minibus. The highlight is viewing a spiritual masked dance that is arranged with the village chief in the morning.

Africa

Africa

Congo

Madagasca

Africa

Congo

The current "Democratic Republic of the Congo" (formally known as Zaire), has had a tumultuous recent history and is currently not recommended for travel. However, the highly inhabited (66 Million) people that populate this Central African country has given its title as the 'most populace country where French is the official language'.

GEOGRAPHY:

- Capital: Kinshasa
- Population: 66 Million

TO-DO:

Please do not visit, unless going with an official tour group or government agency

DISPUTES:

There have been strong factional disputes following Mobutu (president from 1965 until forced into exile in 1997) when he was overthrown by Laurent Kabila, who immediately assumed governing authority. His regime was subsequently challenged by a Rwanda / Uganda backed rebellion in 1998, which led to the one of the bloodiest civil wars in history (second next to WWII) killing 5.4 million people. Congolese politics have also been subjugated by the previous civil war in neighboring Rwanda, including an invasion of refugees that escaped the mass genocide in 1994.

Madagascar

Madagascar, the 4th largest island in the world lays off the southeastern coast of Africa. Eighty percent of plants and animals are indigenous to the island, and not found anywhere else in the world. The people are no less interesting than its landscape. Most come from decedents of Southeast Asia, when the island was first inhabited some 1500 years ago. Though French is one of the three official languages Malagasy, French & English), their dialect has more in common with their origins in Southeast Asia than with the African continent. Madagascar is a beautiful unforgettable place to visit, but please use caution as the political situation is volatile. Please check with the BBC or Safe Travel for updated government warnings.

Best time to visit Sept.-Nov.

GEOGRAPHY:

- Capital: Antananarivo
- Population: 20 Million

TO-DO:

1. Tsingy de Bemaraha Strict Nature Reserve – Explore Tsingy limestone rock formations and view lemurs in this wild park which is celebrated as one of UNESCO's World Herritage Sites
2. Andilana – Watch the sunset on the beautiful Andilana beach.
3. Locals – hang out with the locals and hopefully get in to view one of their religious native practices: dances tell the story between life and death.

Band Bios

RACINE

Band Bios

We searched far and wide to find an eclectic bunch of artists offering some of the best music French-speaking countries have to offer. The french Artists offered on this Compilation are from: France, Canada, Switzerland, and USA.

The following pages include mini-bios of artists featured on the compilation.

- Artist origins
- Website/ Myspace address
- How the artist(s) began their career in music
- Outside influences reflected within the songs

Of course there are many more great artists we couldn't fit onto one compilation. Look into artists from countries that strike your interest. Travel, Listen, Read.... Learn!

The songs the SUBLingual crew seeks out are easy to listen, understandable lyrics and all around feel-good music. Like music from USA (hip-hop, country, classic rock), French music comes in many varieties dependant on the region. As we are becoming a global society, styles of music are blending together. SUBLingual seeks out songs that offer both an international sound with distinct regional flare.

Listen and Learn
about the artists...
If you like them,
seek out more of
their music!

Artist: Jean Racine **Jamming Since: 2006**
Song: Entre Nous **www.myspace.com/jeanracine**
From: born in Sénégal and later moved to Paris, France.

Born in Sénégal, Jean Racine was strongly influenced by the music of Bob Marley and Cat Stevens. He left his native Sénégal to attend college in Paris, but music led him on another path. He began by singing in the streets and eventually met Mehdi Midaoui whose striking voice won him over – he became Mehdi's faithful guitarist. Soon thereafter he met Henry Hirsh, (Lenny Kravitz' producer) who was a great mentor for his future career. Although his work is now produced in Paris and New York, Jean Racine's soul remains in Africa. He writes, "For my first album, I wanted to find the ambiance and the rhythms of the '60s and '70s. His album is inspired by the past, but gives off a resolute modern and international pop feel in what he calls "African Motown."

Artist: Mademoiselle K **Jamming Since: 2005**
Song: Fringue par Fringue **www.mademoisellek.com**
From: Paris, France.

Mademoiselle K evolved out Katerine Gierak's personal passion project. Today the group combines the collective energies of Pierre-Antoine Combard (aka Peter, guitarist), Pierre-Louis Basset (aka Pilou, bassist), Katerine Gierak (singer, guitarist) and David Boutherne (drummer).The song "Fringue par Fringue" is part of the group's most recent album "Jamais La Paix"– produced by Ken Allardyce (Green Day, Weezer) in 2008. Katerine recalls two of Ken's comments: "Your lyrics are weird Katerine, but I like it" and, "I prefer the groove of this take". For the group, "le groove" and "la bizarrerie" are essential elements of their music. With surreal imagery, alternately wild, furious, sarcastic and moody lyrics, Mademoiselle K creates its musical world in the pure spirit of rock, while at the same time puts their own spin on French indie music.

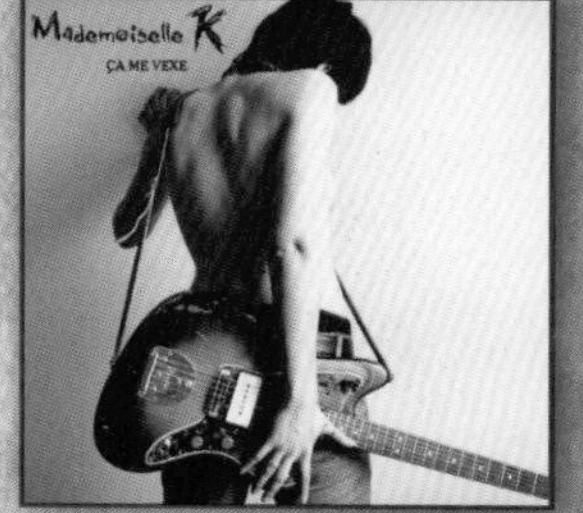

Artist: Marianne Feder **Jamming Since: 2004**
Song: Je Vais Peut-être Attendre Demain **www.mariannefeder.com**
From: Paris, France.

As the daughter of Polish immigrants, Marianne Feder grew up surrounded by jazz. The song featured in this compilation appears on her second album, "Toi Mon Indien". Supported by a colorful team of musicians and their varied instruments, Marianne presents beautiful ballads which evoke the spirit of jazz. In her music, one recognizes several influences – flashes of Kusturica and Tom Waits, the acid brass of Mingus, the deceptive lightness of Bacharach as well as a few masterful nods to a certain French cinema of the 1960s. In short Feder's work is lively and spontaneous, rich and cultivated.

Artist: Emilie Simon **Jamming Since: 2002**
Song: Desert **www.emiliesimon.com**
From: Montpellier, France

Although Emilie Simon is an experimental musician with a strong academic background, she has made a name for herself both as a mainstream composer and as an electronic pop musician. Similar sounds that are compared to her are abstract artists such as Björk, Thievery Corporation or The Knife. With a distinctively soft, almost babyish voice paired with insightful lyrics make up her signature sound. Simon's attractive mixture of art rock and catchy electronic pop was first unveiled on 2003's Emilie Simon, released to positive reviews and eventually winning a Victoire de la Musique (the French equivalent to the Grammy) for best electronica album of the year. Documentary director Luc Jacquet then contacted Simon to score his immersive 2005 nature documentary March of the Penquins. Simon's third album, 2006's Vegetal, not only including lyrics about vegetation but also sampled sounds taken from actual plants.

Artist: Carla Bruni **Jamming Since: 2002**
Songs: Raphael & Quelqu'un m'a dit **www.carlabruni.com**
From: Italy, Switzerland & France

Before fulfilling her childhood dream of becoming a professional singer and songwriter, Carla Bruni had already been included on Business Age's list of the 20 highest-paid models. In addition to appearing in numerous films, she had also gained the spotlight of all tabloids-being romantically linked to mega-stars such as: Mick Jagger, Eric Clapton, Kevin Costner, and Donald Trump. Her fame began when Carla was 19, Paul Marciano – president and creative director of GUESS? – picked Bruni's headshot out of a stack of photographs and turned her into an overnight sensation. In 2003 (in her mid thirties), Bruni made a name for herself upon releasing her debut album hit, Quelqu'un M'a Dit – an instant hit in France, selling one million copies soon after its release. Her second album, "No Promises", appeared in January 2007. Bruni stunned everyone the following year when she became "the First Lady of France" after marrying French President Nicolas Sarkozy in 2008. The most recent appearance was an interview with Barbara Walters touching on the interesting paths her life she has led her. Fans are standing by to see what will come next for the multi-talented First Lady of France.

Artist: Melanie Pain **Jamming Since: 2007**
Song: Celle de mes 20 Ans **www.melaniepain.com**
From: Aix-en-Provence, France

As a young singer/ songwriter herself, Melanie sings many songs relating to the growing up experiences of the early twenties. Widely associated by singing alongside popular Nouvelle Vague and Villeneuve in France, Mélanie has recently released her solo album in 2009 with "My Name". Hailing from Aix-en-Provence in France, she cites influences that include Sonic Youth, the Smiths, Pixies, PJ Harvey, and Nick Drake. Young, creative and offering a fresh sound to French music, fans are eagerly awaiting more to come from this new face in music.

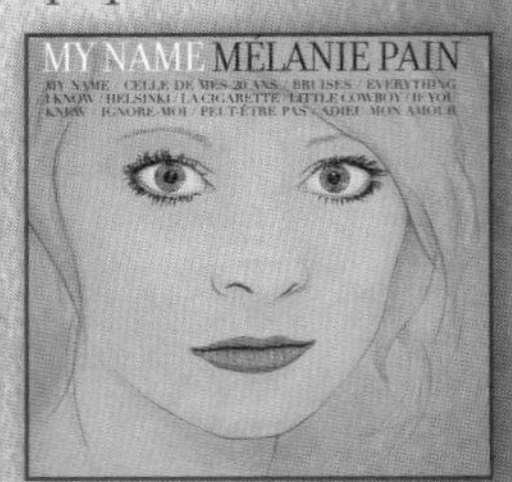

Artist: Coralie Clement **Jamming Since: 2002**
Song: C' est La Vie **www.myspace.com/coralieclment**
From: Villefranche-sur-Saône, France

Well know in France as the young, fresh artist on the rise of popularity. Coralie's sound is unique yet encompasses the the classic '60s French pop sound such as her influencers – Jane Birkin and Francoise Hardy. She was no stranger to talent, as she was born into a musical family and thus spawned an interest in her at an early age. Coralie could identify all of the instruments of the orchestra by the age of three, studied musical theory at five, and at six, she took up the violin. Coralie's brother (famous French musician Benjamin Biolay) both inspired and helped her begin her own career with her new album "Salle des Pas Perdus" in 2002. Ironically, what she is most known for – her voice – she never considered herself to be good at. Her lyrics are both reflective and relatable which has made her a pop sensation amongst the "twenty-somethings" in France.

Artist: Housse De Racket **Jamming since: 2006**
Song: 1,2,3,4 **http://www.myspace.com/houssederacket**
From: Paris, France

"Winners of runs, losers in love" is the leitmotiv of Housse de Racket. The roots of their name stem from a love of sport between two childhood friends devoted to tennis. That explains their pick of band name (literally translated as 'racket cover') – was much more than a reference to tennis, rather their way of signaling their aim to make a 'racket' of house music itself. The duo has known each other since their teenage years and started playing music together in class. Compiling numerous songs, the group was inspired to wipe the slate clean and go down a fresh new direction. Mixed with a techno-house yet 60's French rock flair, their sound has caught the attention of Gonzales and Renaud Letang (Feist, Gonzales, Peaches and Manu Chao) who subsequently produced their debut album "Forty Love". Most of their songs offer a wide range of interpretation for the listener to decipher, since most lyrics can be taken into various contexts and meanings.

Artist: Oliver Libaux (featuring Barbara Carlotti)
Song: Le Petit Success **Jamming Since: 1990's**
From: Paris, France **www.myspace.com/nouvellevague**

Oliver Libaux is no rookie to the music scene. As a producer, singer and songwriter he's been around the block and made as many artists stars as he has done for himself. As he chose the name for his album title 'Imbecile' meaning: " One who walks without a stick, who learns to walk without crutches at the risk of committing mistakes and falling, but nevertheless keeps moving forward allowing that person to progress". Oliver's music exceeds his modest take on life. As major contributor to collaboration band "Novelle Vague" (created by both Libaux and producer Marc Collin). Nouvelle Vague has spawned numerous careers for other artists such as Melanie Pain, Camille and Barbara Carlotti- who happens to be the singer on this track.

Artist: Amelia **Jamming Since: 2003**
Song: Et Vous **www.ameliaband.com**
From: Portland, Oregon USA

Surprising that an "All-American" band can put out such great French music. Amelia's band-members from Portland, Oregon are a hodgepodge of cool hipsters all originating from individual musical backgrounds. This collective group started off with 2, then 5 then now currently at 4 members. The common denominators of the band (Teisha and Scott – singer and drummer, respectively) have picked up musical talent along the way picking up great talent on the road. Amelia members have performed with well-known artists such as the Decemberists, M. Ward and Elliott Smith… More to come from these guys and hopefully more songs in French!

Artist: Francoiz Breut **Jamming Since: 1997**
Song: La Cerlitude **www.myspace.com/francoizbreut**
From: Cherbourg, France

In the '90s, singer Francoiz Breut established herself as an important player on the French music scene. Breut, who is known for melancholy, introspective lyrics and a smoky, jazz-tinged approach to pop-rock, has inspired a variety of comparisons such as '60s ye-ye icon Françoise Hardy or German singer Nico. Occasionally, Breut has embraced English-language material (such as "My Wedding Man" from her self-titled debut album), but more often than not, her material has been in French. And while the language barrier prevented her from becoming well known in the United States in the '90s, it wasn't as much of an issue in Europe (where people are more likely to become fluent in several languages). Francoiz has laid low on the releasing any new music in the past few years, but her music remains a keepsake to French music-lovers everywhere.

Artist: Pink Martini **Jamming Since: 1994**
Song: O Est Ma Tete **www.pinkmartini.com**
From: Portland, Oregon USA

Pink Martini is the epitome of "World Music" for the real meaning of the category. The band from Portland, Oregon is comprised of 12 members all from various cultural backgrounds as the music resonates from the first listen. China Forbes (singer) has performed in at least ten different languages and is fluent in four. Founder/pianist Thomas Lauderdale states about their unique style "all of us in the band have studied different languages and music from different parts of the world, so inevitably, because everyone in the band contributes in the writing and arranging of songs, the repertoire is wildly diverse. At one moment, you feel like you're in the middle of a samba parade in Rio de Janeiro, and in the next moment, you are suddenly in a French music hall of the 1930s or in a palazzo in Napoli. It's like an urban musical travelogue." "We're very much an American band and have the rare opportunity to represent a different kind of America through our repertoire and our concerts – that is, an America which is the most heterogeneously populated country in the world – comprised of people from every country, every language, every religion." "One of our goals is to make music which has broad appeal to people, no matter who they are or where they come from. We play the same set of music wherever we go, whether it's in a small farming community in Oregon or in France or Turkey or with a symphony orchestra. My hope is that we're creating music which can be turned up or down, and played on almost any occasion, from background music of a love affair to vacuuming around the house."

Lauderdale did a great job at summing up the bands global outlook by stating: "I think it's important to be a citizen of the world as opposed to being a citizen of this particular country. Part of that means studying other people's languages." (– and yes, we agree!)

Toystore
Coralie Clément
carla
bruni
quel
THIS WAY
THAT WAY

Lyrics

vie
vie qu'on mène
assant ne nous renseigne
vie
vie cette chienne
qu'on restera nous-même
vie
vie quand même
as vilain, l'Ille-et-Vilaine
a vie
a vie qu'on mène

J'ai déserté les alentours
Je te quitte, voilà c'est tou
Dans la nuit parfois, le nez
J'attendais et

Tout peut chavirer autour
Il y a la certitude de tes yeux
Qui portent tout cet amour
Sans relâche je sonde
Ses petites profondeurs rien de plus à desirer
Que 2 lacs voilés
Les yeux dans les yeux et rien d'autre

uatre consonnes et trois
yelles
est le prénom de Raphaël
le murmure à mon oreille
chaque lettre m'émerveille
st le tréma qui
nsorcelle
s le prénom de Raphaël
me il se mêle au a au e
me il les entre-mêle au l
ël, à l'air d'un ange
c'est un diable de
ur
ut des hanches
son regard de velours
il se penche
il se penche mes nuits
anches
ur toujours

Quand je pense à toi, je ne
pense à rien
Tu m'ennuies tu ne sais pas
Ô combien
Fidèle comme un nombre, je
marchais au pas
Du neuf sous les décombres,
je marcherai droit
Sur les boulevards je t'évite
Tu es la boule noire, le numéro huit
Toi et moi c'est simple, c'est
comme 1 2 3

Soleil qui
m'éblouissait
Brille encore les
jours du beau
temps
Mais c'est quand
les vents forts ont
soufflé
Que j'ai dû y
laisser des

Je crois que j'vais peut-être attendre demain
Pour devenir quelqu'un de bien

On me dit que nos vies ne va

Il est arrivé
Il a tout changé
Le petit succès
Dès qu'il s'est pointé
Il a tout transformé
Le petit succès
Et moi j'en ai bavé
Au mois de juillet
Pendant que t'avais
Ton petit succès

Entre nous c'était fort
T'entends même plus quand je t'implore
Pourquoi l'amour nous mène-t-il à ce triste sort?
Entre nous c'est bien mort
Entre nous
L'histoire retiendra mes larmes
Entre nous c'était fort

Je pourrais même tout arracher
Te coincer entre deux portes
Oh! Et que le diable m'emporte...

Je pourrais même bien t'attacher
Te garder là à mes bottes
Oui! Que le diable m'emporte...

nous
Qu'il ne nous donne rien et

Carla Bruni

Raphaël

Enamored with her lover, the singer finds how perfect he is through all of his uniqueness and explains why thru the fundamentals of his name "Raphael".

Quatre consonnes et trois voyelles
Three consonants and three vowels

C'est le prénom de Raphaël
It's the first name Raphaël

Je le murmure à mon oreille
I murmur it to myself

Et chaque lettre m'émerveille
and each letter amazes me

C'est le tréma qui m'ensorcelle
It's the diaeresis accent which captivates me

Dans le prénom de Raphaël
In the first name Raphaël

Comme il se mêle au a au e
As it blends with the "a" and "e"

Comme il les entre-mêle au l
As it interweaves them with the "l"

Raphaël à l'air d'un ange
He seems like an angel

Mais c'est un diable de l'amour
But he is a devil in love

Du bout des hanches
From the end of his hips

Et de son regard de velours
And his velvet stare

Quand il se penche
When he leans (over me)

Quand il se penche mes nuits sont blanches
When he leans (over me) I'm up all night

Et pour toujours
And forever

Hmm
Hmm

J'aime les notes au goût de miel
I like the honeyed notes

Dans le prénom de Raphaël
In the first name Raphaël

Je les murmure à mon réveil
I murmur them when I'm waking up

Entre les plumes du sommeil
Between the feathers of sleep

Et pour que la journée soit belle
And so that the day will be beautiful

Je me parfume à Raphaël
I perfume myself with Raphaël

Peau de chagrin peintre eternel
Skin of sorrow, eternal painter

Bio on page 19
Track 1 2:23

Archange étrange d'un autre ciel
Strange archangel from another heaven

Pas de délices pas d'étincelle
No delight, no spark

Pas de malice sans Raphaël
No mischief without Raphaël

Les jours sans lui deviennent ennui
Days without him become boring

Et mes nuits s'ennuient de plus belle
And my nights grow even more boring

Pas d'inquiétude pas de prélude
No anxiety no prelude

Pas de promesses à l'éternel
No eternal promises

Juste l'amour dans notre lit
Just the world in our bed

Juste nos vies en arc-en-ciel
Just our lives in rainbows

Raphaël a l'air d'un sage
Raphaël seems like a sage

Et ses paroles sont de velours
And his words are velvet

De sa voix grave
Of his solemn voice

Et de son regard sans détours
And of his direct look

Quand il raconte
When he tells stories

Quand il invente je peux l'écouter
When he invents I can listen to him

Nuit et jour
Night and day

Hmm
Hmm

Quatre consonnes et trois voyelles
Four consonants and three vowels

C'est le prénom de Raphaël
That's the first name Raphaël

Je lui murmure à son oreille
I murmur it into his ear

Ca le fait rire comme un soleil
It makes him laugh like a sun.

Marianne Feder

Je vais attendre peut-être demain – Maybe I'm going to wait until tomorrow

Moi, j'voudrais faire du cinéma
I'd like to make movies

Être cantatrice à l'opéra
Be an opera singer

Chanter du jazz comme Sinatra
Sing Jazz like Sinatra

Être divine comme une diva
Be divine like a diva

Faire des claquettes et du yoga
Tap dance and do yoga

Apprendre le serbe et le chinois
Learn Serbian and Chinese

Faire la guérilla au Chiapas
Be a guerrilla fighter in Chiapas

Écrire un livre sur Mandela
Write a book on Mandela

À côté d'ça, qu'est-ce que c'est bon
Aside from that, how nice it is

D'rester près de toi sous l'édredon
To stay next to you under the comforter

Je crois que j'vais peut-être attendre demain
I think I might wait until tomorrow

Pour devenir quelqu'un de bien
To become someone good

Je crois que j'vais peut-être attendre demain
I think I might wait until tomorrow

Pour devenir quelqu'un de bien
To become someone good

J'voudrais être la star d'aujourd'hui
I want to be today's star

Qu'on m'applaudisse quand je sors du lit
And have everyone applaud when I get out of bed

Avoir la classe et des amis
To have class and friends

Faire du roller tous les Samedis
To go rollerblading every Saturday

Avoir un agenda booké
Have a booked schedule

Être présente à toutes les soirées
Attend all the parties

Rire et guincher toute la nuit
Laugh and dance all night long

Finir à l'aube en bikini
End up at dawn in a bikini

A common goal is to excel and succeed in life at becoming great at something, but sometimes, it is the simple pleasures in life (like being with the one you love) that is the most rewarding.

Bio on page 18
Track 2 3:37

À côté d'ça j'aime faire la gueule
Aside form that I like to keep quiet

J'ai pas beaucoup d'conversation
I'm not much into conversation

J'aime pas la foule, j'suis pas mondaine
I don't like crowds, I'm not a socialite

Je préfère la chambre au salon
I prefer the bedroom to the parlor

Je crois que j'vais peut-être attendre demain
I think I might wait until tomorrow

Pour devenir quelqu'un de bien
To become someone good

J'aimerais traverser l'Atlantique
I'd like to cross the Atlantic

En solitaire sur un voilier
Solo on a sailboat

Découvrir le nouveau vaccin
Discover a new vaccine

Qui éradiquerait la faim
Which would eradicate hunger

Être reporter, pilote de l'air
Be a reporter, an airplane pilot

Vivre en ermite sur un rocher
Live like a hermit on a rock

Faire l'tour du monde en montgolfière
Take a trip around the world in a hot air balloon

Devenir bouddhiste et méditer
Become a Buddhist and meditate

J'aimerais renverser la planète et dire bonjour avec les pieds
I'd like to turn the planet upside down and say hello with my feet

Peut-être qu'en marchant sur la tête, j'trouverais le monde un peu moins
Maybe by walking on my hands, I might find the world a little less

Bête
Stupid

Moi je veux devenir quelqu'un de mature et d'indépendant
I want to become someone mature and independent

Aventurière, une guerrière, une figure révolutionnaire.
An adventurer, a fighter, a revolutionary figure.

En même temps je déteste être seule
At the same time I hate being alone

J'ai pas d'génie j'ai pas la foi
I'm no genius I have no faith

Dans mon coeur y a que de l'amour
There is only love in my heart

Et l'bout du monde m'éloigne de toi
And the ends of the earth distance me from you

→

Je vais attendre peut-être demain – Maybe I'm ging to wait until tomorrow

Dans mon coeur y a que de l'amour
There is only love in my heart

Et l'bout du monde m'éloigne de toi
And the ends of the earth distance me from you

J'crois que je vais laisser l'conditionnel
I think I'm going to leave the conditional

Rêver pour moi vers les étoiles
And dream for myself in the stars

Et peut-être qu'un jour mine de rien
And maybe one day worn down by nothing

Je deviendrais quel'qu'un de bien
I (would / will) become someone good

Quelqu'un de bien...
Someone good...

J'crois que je vais laisser l'conditionnel
I think I'm going to leave the conditional

Rêver pour moi vers les étoiles
And reach for the stars

Et peut-être qu'un jour mine de rien
And maybe one day without being obvious

Je deviendrais quel'qu'un de bien
I might become someone good

Housse de Racket
1-2-3-4

Bio on page 20
Track 3 2:52

Quand je pense à toi, je ne pense à rien
When I think about you I don't think about anything

Tu m'ennuies tu ne sais pas ô combien
You don't know how much you annoy me

Fidèle comme un nombre, je marchais au pas
Faithful like a number, I used to walk in the footsteps

Du neuf sous les décombres, je marcherai droit
Of the nine under the rubble, I will walk upright

Sur les boulevards je t'évite
On the boulevards I avoid you

Tu es la boule noire, le numéro huit
You're the black ball, the number eight

Toi et moi c'est simple, c'est comme 1 2 3 4
You and me it's simple, it's like 1 2 3 4

Mais toi tu prends la fuite comme 5 6 7 8
But you run away like 5 6 7 8

Quand tu penses à moi, je ne compte pas
When you think about me, I don't count

Je suis ordinaire, numéro complémentaire
I am ordinary, a complementary number

Désormais le deux, c'est fini
From now on the two is done.

Vive le un, vive l'ennui
Long live the one, long live boredom

Trop de toi sur les trottoirs
Too much of you on the sidewalks

Trop d'amour sur les faubourgs
Too much love in the outskirts of town

Je parle seul toutes les nuits
I talk by myself every night

Je suis le rapporteur de Paris
I am the informant from Paris

Toi et moi c'est simple, c'est comme 1 2 3 4
You and me it's simple, it's like 1 2 3 4

Mais toi tu prends la fuite comme 5 6 7 8
But you run away like 5 6 7 8

Toi et moi c'est simple, c'est comme 1 2 3 4
You and me it's simple, it's like 1 2 3 4

Mais moi je prends la fuite comme 5 6 7 8
But I run away like 5 6 7 8

A common experience for young people in "love" the singer is frustrated with his relationship since every time he steps closer, she pushes away. In the closing of the song, he is as guilty as she, as denoted by the last line in the song "..I run away like 5,6,7,8".

Coralie Clément

C'est La Vie – That's life

A humble perspective on the intricacies of life and not having everything always going as planned. Her resolution is not to be mad, but that life's problems "forces us to stay ourselves".

C'est la vie
That's life

C'est la vie qu'on mène
It's the life one leads

Aucun passant ne nous renseigne
No passerby tells us how to (lead it)

C'est la vie
That's life

C'est la vie cette chienne
It's this wretched life

Qui fait qu'on restera nous-même
Which forces us to stay ourselves

C'est la vie
That's life

C'est la vie quand même
It's life all the same

C'est pas vilain, l'Ille-et-Vilaine
It's not that ugly, Ille and Vilaine

C'est la vie
That's life

C'est la vie qu'on mène
It's the life one leads

Anxiolytiques et café crème
anti-anxiety pills and café-crème

La vie qui brûle nos idoles
The life which burns our idols

Une grue dans la cour de l'école
A crane in the courtyard of the school

C'est la vie
That's life

C'est la vie qu'on mène
It's the life one leads

On baigne dans son sang tout baigne
We bathe in it's blood, everything bathes in it

C'est la vie
That's life

C'est la vie quand même
It's life all the same

On voudrait boire l'eau des fontaines
We'd like to drink water from the fountains

C'est la vie
That's life

C'est la vie bohème
It's the bohemian life

Bio on page 19
Track 4   2:28

La nuit qu'on préfère les enseigne
The night we prefer teaches them

C'est la vie
That's life

C'est la vie cette chienne
It's this wretched life

Il est grand temps qu'on se renseigne
It's about time we figure things out

La vie qui brûle nos idoles
The life which burns our idols

Comme l'été brûle l'herbe folle
Like the summer burns the wild grasses

Moi je n'oublie pas
Me, I don't forget

Nos premiers pas
Our first steps

Je n'oublie pas non plus
I also don't forget

Le premier clash
The first clash

Les premiers mots crus
The first harsh words

Et cette paire de claques
And that pair of slaps

Sur le clic clac
On the sofa bed

Je cours dans les flaques
I run in the puddles

C'est la vie
That's life

C'est la vie cette chienne
It's this wretched life

Francoiz Breut

La Certitude – Certainty

Tout peut chavirer autour
Everything may reel around me

Il y a la certitude de tes yeux
There is the certainty of your eyes

Qui portent tout cet amour
Which carry all this love

Sans relâche je sonde
Relentlessly I probe

Ses petites profondeurs rien de plus à desirer
Their small depths, desiring nothing more

Que 2 lacs voilés
Than two veiled lakes

Les yeux dans les yeux et rien d'autre
Gazing into each others eyes and nothing more

Le premier regard me remplit
The first look fills me

Comme si tout le reste m'était étranger
As if all the rest were unfamiliar to me

Tout peut chavirer autour
Everything may reel around me

Il y a la certitude de tes yeux
There is the certainty of your eyes

Qui portent tout cet amour
Which carry all of this love

Sans relâche je sonde
Tirelessly I probe

Ses petites profondeurs rien de plus à desirer
Its small depths, desiring nothing more

Que 2 lacs voilés
Than two veiled lakes

Les yeux dans les yeux et rien d'autre
Gazing into each others eyes and nothing more

Le premier regard me remplit
The first look fills me

Comme si tout le reste m'était étranger
As if all the rest were unfamiliar to me

Adorned lovers find the pleasure of gazing into one another's eyes while realizing their eyes is the deepest connection they can have between them.

Bio on page 21
Track 5 3:23

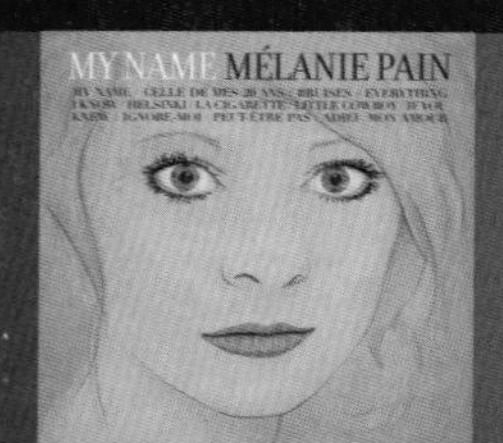

Mélanie Pain

Celle de mes vingt ans – My twenty year old self

(Pap Deziel/Benoît Villeneuve

Le soleil qui m'éblouissait
The sun which used to dazzle me

Brille encore les jours du beau temps
Still shines on the nice days

Mais c'est quand les vents forts ont soufflé
But it was when the strong winds blew

Que j'ai dû y laisser des dents
that I had to endure the most hardship

Et quand la pluie a redoublé
And when the rain intensified

Mes yeux se sont troublés souvent
My eyes would often blur

refrain

C'est vrai que je ne suis plus
It's true that I'm no longer

Celle que j'étais
the one I used to be

Est-ce moi qui ai changé
Am I the one who changed

Qui ai vraiment changé
Who really changed

Je ne suis plus celle que j'étais
I am no longer the one I used to be

Mais suis-je meilleure plus va le temps
But am I better as more time passes by

Suis-je une femme ou une fille qui essaie
Am I a woman or a girl who tries

Et qui échoue lamentablement
And who fails miserably

Et mon regard dans le miroir
And my eyes in the mirror

Est-il plus profond à présent
Are they more profound now

Peut-être est-il un peu plus noir
Maybe they are a little darker

Depuis qu'il ne s'ouvre plus en grand
Since they are no longer opened wide

Voudrais-tu celle de mes vingt ans
Would you like the 20 year old I was

Aller, danser avec moi maintenant
Come, dance with me now

With the passing into her twenties a pivotal moment is reached as the singer feels she is growing into adulthood. She feels deeper, less naïve than when she was a young girl but questions if it was her that changed or just everything around her?

Bio on page 19
Track 6 3:18

C'est vrai que je ne suis plus
It's true that I'm no longer

Celle que j'étais
the one I used to be

Est-ce moi qui ai changé
Am I the one who changed

Qui ai changé vraiment
Who really changed

Ou est-ce tout le reste
Or is it everything else

Qui a foutu le camp
Which disappeared

Mes rues, mes amis d'avant, et celle de mes vingt ans
My streets, my friends from before and my 20 year old self

refrain

C'est vrai que je ne suis plus
It's true that I'm no longer

Celle que j'étais
The one I used to be

Est-ce moi qui ai changé
Am I the one who changed

Qui ai changé vraiment
Who really changed

Oliver Libaux & Barbara Carlott

Le Petit Succès – The Little Success

The ups and downs of gaining success and reaching ones goals are a rollercoaster filled with a humbling experience. Though you get what you want, you still fall back down to begin the process once again.

Depuis le temps que t'en rêvais
Since the time when you used to dreamt about it

Il est arrivé
It happened

Il a tout changé
It changed everything

Le petit succès
The little success

Depuis le temps que t'en rêvais
Since the time you used to dream about it

Dés qu'il s'est pointé
As soon as it turned up

Il a tout transformé
It transformed everything

Le petit succès
The little success

Et moi j'en ai bavé
And I had a hard time with it

Au mois de juillet
In the month of July

Pendant que t'avais
While you were having

Ton petit succès
Your little success

Mais il n'a pas duré
But it didn't last

Plus d'un seul été
More than a single Summer

Il est retombé
It fell back down

Le petit succès
The little success

E moi je n'ai pas bougé
And I didn't move

Quand le temps a changé
When the weather changed

Et qu'à bout de succès
And at the end of the success

T'as fini par tomber
You ended up falling

Oh non je n'ai pas bougé
Oh no I didn't move

Car le vent a tourné
Because the wind changed

Et là c'était mon tour
And then it was my turn

D'avoir du succès
To succeed

Bio on page 20
Track 7 3:13

Les ailes déployées
My wings outstretched

Et le cœur léger
And my heart light

Je me suis grisée
I got drunk on

De petit succès
the little success.

Mais je suis retombée
But I fell back down

Peu de temps après
After a little while

Le petit succès
The little success

Ne m'a pas épargnée
Did not spare me

Et alors je t'ai cherché
And so I looked for you

Et je t'ai retrouvé
And I found you again

Il nous avait changés
It changed us

Le petit succès
The little success

Il nous avait changés
It changed us

Au coin qu'on s'est croisé
At the corner where we met

Et que nos yeux blessés
And with our wounded eyes

On ne pourrait plus s'aimer
We couldn't love each other anymore

Vu le mal qu'il nous fait
Given the harm it has done to us

Il faut s'en méfier
We must we wary of

Du petit succès
Of little success

Dès qu'il apparaît
As soon as it appears

Mais on aime tant souffrir
But we love to suffer greatly

Rêve de voler
Dream of flying

Et qu'on peut résister
And than we can resist

A l'appel du succès
The call of success

Pink Martini

Où Est ma tête? – Where is my head?

A cute allegorical song about losing your head, limbs or appendages as the way one feels when they lost the one that matters most. None of her body parts are needed, as long as she has her love to complete her.

J'ai perdu ma tête
I lost my head

Dans la rue Saint Honoré
On Saint Honoré street

J'ai cherché ça et là
I looked here and there

Je ne l'ai pas trouvée
I didn't find it

Dis moi – Où est ma tête?
Tell me – where is my head?

J'ai perdu mes bras
I lost my arms

Sur la Place de l'Opéra
At the Place de l'Opera

Je n'les ai pas trouvés
I didn't find them

J'ai cherché ça et là
I looked here and there

Dis moi – Où sont mes bras?
Tell me – Where are my arms?

Depuis que je t'ai perdu
Since I lost you

Je suis en pièces sur l'avenue
I am in pieces on the avenue

Et je ne peux pas recoller les morceaux par moi-même
And I can't glue the pieces back together by myself

Répare-moi, mon très cher
Repair me, my darling

Parce que je ne suis pas entière
Because I am not whole

J'ai besoin de toi – seulement toi –
I need you – only you –

Et en plus… je t'aime
And furthermore... I love you

J'ai perdu mon nez
I lost my nose

Devant le Bon Marché
In front of the Bon Marché

J'ai cherché ça et là
I looked here and there

Je ne l'ai pas trouvé
I didn't find it

Dis moi – Où est mon nez?
Tell me – where is my nose?

Bio on page 21
Track 8 4:16

Reviens cheri vers moi
Come back to me darling

Mon nez n'importe pas
My nose doesn't matter

C'est toi qui peux me compléter
It's you who can complete me

Depuis que je t'ai perdu
Since I lost you

Je suis en pièces sur l'avenue
I am in pieces on the avenue

Et je ne peux pas recoller les morceaux par moi-même
And I can't glue the pieces back together by myself

Répare-moi, mon très cher
Repair me, my darling

Parce que je ne suis pas entière
Because I am not whole

J'ai besoin de toi
I need you

Et en plus… je t'aime
And furthermore... I love you

J'ai perdu mes pieds
I lost my feet

Au Saint Germain des Près
At Saint Germain des Près

J'ai cherché ça et là
I looked here and there

Je n'les ai pas trouvés
I didn't find them

Dis moi – Où sont mes pieds?
Tell me – where are my feet?

Reviens cheri, vers moi
Come back to me darling

Mes pieds n'importent pas
My feet don't matter

C'est toi qui peux me compléter
It's you who can complete me

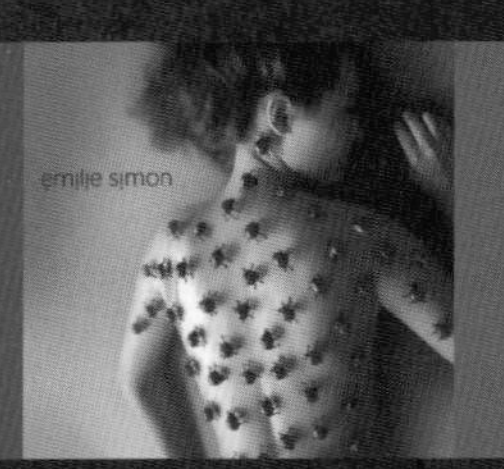

Emilie Simon

Désert – Desert

The calling for a missed soul mate, she is yearning to fill the "desert" or void in her heart that has resulted in ones absence. She counts the days and hours that go by until their return.

Oh mon amour, mon âme-soeur
Oh my love, my soul mate

Je compte les jours je compte les heures
I count the days I count the hours

Je voudrais te dessiner dans un désert
I'd like to draw you in a desert

Le désert de mon coeur
The desert of my heart

Oh mon amour, ton grain de voix
Oh my love, the texture of your voice

Fait mon bonheur à chaque pas
Makes me happy with each step

Laisse-moi te dessiner dans un désert
Let me draw you in a desert

Le désert de mon coeur
The desert of my heart

Dans la nuit parfois, le nez à la fenêtre
Sometimes at night, with my nose to the window

Je t'attends et je sombre
I wait for you and I'm sinking

Dans un désert, dans mon désert, voilà
In a desert, in my desert, that's it

Oh mon amour, mon coeur est lourd
Oh my love, my heart is heavy

Je compte les heures je compte les jours
I count the hours I count the days

Je voudrais te dessiner dans un désert
I'd like to draw you in a desert

Le désert de mon coeur
The desert of my heart

Oh mon amour, je passe mon tour
Oh my love, I missed my turn

J'ai déserté les alentours
I deserted the surroundings

Je te quitte, voilà c'est tout...
I'm leaving you, well that's it...

Bio on page 18
Track 9   3:06

Dans la nuit parfois, le nez à la fenêtre
Sometimes at night, with my nose at the window

J'attendais et je sombre
I waited and I'm sinking

Jetez au vent mes tristes cendres, voilà...
Throw my sad ashes to the wind, that's it...

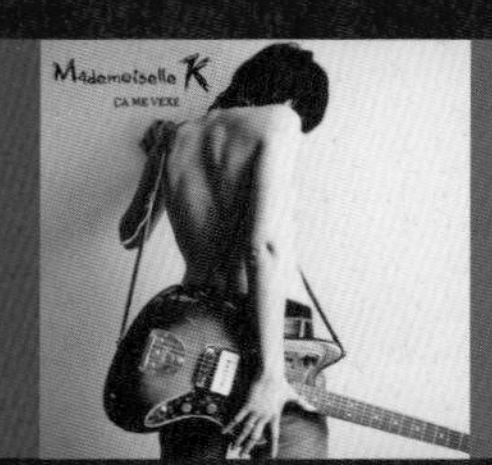

Mademoiselle K (Katrine Gierak

Fringue par Fringue... – Piece by Piece...(of Clothing

Mademoiselle K is known for obscure lyrics, and this song is no exception. She is obsessing about a previous love with someone who has left. She fanaticizes about them being close to her by taking off his clothes 'piece by piece' and keeping them close to her. The singer misses the person and knows that this obsession is unhealthy and sinful, hence, "May the devil take me away."

Fringue par fringue je retire tout ce qui est de trop
Piece by piece I take off anything that is too much

Sur toi
On you

Je pourrais même tout arracher
I could even tear everything off

Te coincer entre deux portes
Wedge you between 2 doors

Oh! Et que le diable m'emporte...
Oh! May the devil carry me away...

refrain (2)

Da lé la ding
Da lé la lé la lé la ding

Viens par là que je me fasse mon cinéma à moi
Come here so I can make my movie

Sur toi
On you

Je pourrais même bien t'attacher
I could even attach you

Te garder là à mes bottes
And keep you there on my boots

Oui! Que le diable m'emporte...
Yes! May the devil take me away...

Que le diable nous emporte...
May the devil take us away...

refrain

Regarde comme tu me manques
See how much I miss you

Je fantasme nuit et jour
I fantasize night and day

A force de plus faire l'amour
Because of not making love anymore
Regarde comme tu me manques
See how much I miss you

Je fantasme nuit et jour
I fantasize night and day

A force de plus faire l'amour
Because of not making love anymore

Bio on page 18
Track 10 4:24

Regarde comme tu me manques (2)
See how much I miss you

Je fantasme nuit et jour (4)
I fantasize night and day

Regarde comme tu me manques
See how much I miss you

Je fantasme nuit et jour (2)
I fantasize night and day

Regarde comme tu me manques
See how much I miss you

Je fantasme nuit et jour
I fantasize night and day

A force de plus faire l'amour
because of not making love anymore

Jean Racine

Entre Nous – Between us

Dans ma tête c'est flou
In my head it's unfocused

Je cherche le nord
I'm looking for the north

Pourquoi le temps est si doux
Why is the weather so mild

Et que tout s'évapore
And (why is) everything disappearing

Entre vous une histoire secrète
Between you, a secret story

Entre nous une flamme qui s'éteint
Between us a flame that is going out

Entre vous des roses qu'on s'achète
Between you roses that you buy for each other

Je reste sur ma faim
I stay with my hunger

Tout d'un coup, un beau jour
All of a sudden, one fine day

L'extase que l'on m'enlève
The ecstasy is taken from me

Entre nous c'est bien mort
Between us it's completely dead

Entre nous
Between us

L'histoire retiendra mes larmes
The story will hold back my tears

Entre nous c'était fort
Between us it was strong

En dehors de nous,
Outside of us,

Je suis vulnérable, je suis sans armes
I'm vulnerable, I'm unarmed

Je suis seul
I'm alone

Je ne suis plus aimé
I'm not loved anymore

Je suis seul
I'm alone

Je récolte ce qu je n'ai pas semé
I reap what I did not sow

refrain (2)

Entre nous les coeurs se crèvent
Between us our hearts are breaking

Entre nous l'histoire s'achève
Between us the story is coming to an end

Entre nous l'histoire se repète
Between us the story repeats itself

Au mépris du lendemain
Regardless of the next day

Entre nous ça part en sucette
Between us things are falling apart

Recalling the empty space "between us" the singer is recognizing the heartbreaking reality between two lovers that have decided to go down separate paths.

Bio on page 17
Track 11 3:16

Chacun poursuit son chemin
Each person pursues their path

Sans trop de remous
Without much turmoil

Mais moi j'en crève
But me, I'm dying from it

Entre nous c'est bien mort
Between us it's completely dead

Entre nous
Between us

L'histoire retiendra mes larmes
The story will hold back my tears

Entre nous c'était fort
Between us it was strong

En dehors de nous,
Outside of us,

Je suis vulnérable, je suis sans armes
I'm vulnerable, I'm unarmed

refrain (2)

Entre nous c'est bien mort
Between us it's completely dead

Entre nous c'était fort
Between us it was strong

T'entends même plus quand je t'implore
You don't hear me any more when I beg you

Pourquoi l'amour nous mène-t-il à ce triste sort?
Why does love lead us to this sad fate?

Entre nous c'est bien mort
Between us it's completely dead

Entre nous
Between us

L'histoire retiendra mes larmes
The story will hold back my tears

Entre nous c'était fort
Between us it was strong

En dehors de nous,
Outside of us,

Je suis vulnérable, je suis sans armes
I'm vulnerable, I'm unarmed

Je suis seul, je ne suis plus aimé
I am alone, I am not loved any more

Je suis seul, je recolte ce que j'ai pas semé
I am alone, I reap what I did not sow

Je suis seul, je ne puis plus aimer
I am alone, I can't love any more

Je suis seul, ça me revolte, je l'aurai pas mérité
I am alone, it appals me, I probably didn't deserve this

refrain (2)

Amelia

Et vous – And you

Pense à la fin
Think about the end

Pas plus à moi
Not about me anymore

Laisse-moi tomber
Let me go

Qu'est-ce que c'est?
What is it?

Ne me regarde comme ça
Don't look at me like that

Sans sens, sans doute
Without meaning, without doubt

Je raconte tout
I tell all

Cette femme et vous
This woman and you

J'avais mes doutes mais puis
I had my doubts but then

Pour lui je suis
For him I am

Si folle, si folle pour lui
So crazy, so crazy for him

J'avais mes doutes mais puis, pour lui
I had my doubts but then, for him

Je suis
I am

Si folle, si folle pour lui
So crazy, so crazy for him

The singer simply declares that she is crazy for her ex love. Even though things may have turned bad between them-- a suspected affair ("This woman and you, I had my doubts") and the approaching break-up, the singer is still crazy for him no matter what.

Bio on page 20
Track 12 2:27

Carla Bruni

Quelqu'un m'a dit – Someone told me

"Someone told me that you still love me? Could it be possible" she continually asks herself. Though she can't remember who had told her this rumor, she hopes it is true as she realizes time slips away as fast as roses fade.

On me dit que nos vies ne valent pas grand chose
People tell me that our lives aren't worth much

Elles passent en un instant comme fanent les roses
They go by in an instant the way roses fade.

On me dit que le temps qui glisse est un salaud
People tell me that the time which slips by is a bastard

Que de nos chagrins il s'en fait des manteaux
Who clothes himself in our sorrows

Pourtant quelqu'un m'a dit...
And yet someone told me...

Que tu m'aimais encore,
That you still loved me,

C'est quelqu'un qui m'a dit que tu m'aimais encore.
Someone told me that you still loved me.

Serait-ce possible alors?
Could it be possible?

On me dit que le destin se moque bien de nous
People tell me that destiny mocks us

Qu'il ne nous donne rien et qu'il nous promet tout
That it gives us nothing and promises us everything.

Paraît que le bonheur est à portée de main,
It seems like happiness is just an arms' reach away,

Alors on tend la main et on se retrouve fou
So we reach out with our hand and end up going crazy

Pourtant quelqu'un m'a dit...
And yet, someone told me...

Que tu m'aimais encore,
That you still loved me,

C'est quelqu'un qui m'a dit que tu m'aimais encore.
Someone told me that you still loved me.

Serait-ce possible alors?
Could it be possible?

Serait-ce possible alors?
Could it be possible?

Bio on page 19
Track 13 2:46

Mais qui est-ce qui m'a dit que toujours tu m'aimais?
But who told me that you still loved me?

Je ne me souviens plus c'était tard dans la nuit,
I don't remember any more, it was late at night,

J'entends encore la voix, mais je ne vois plus les traits
I still hear the voice, but I can't make out the features

"Il vous aime, c'est secret,
lui dites pas que j'vous l'ai dit"
"He loves you, it's a secret, don't tell him I told you"

Tu vois quelqu'un m'a dit...
You see, someone told me...

Que tu m'aimais encore, me l'a t'on vraiment dit...
That you still loved me, did they really tell me...

Que tu m'aimais encore, serait-ce possible alors?
That you still loved me, could it be possible?

On me dit que nos vies ne valent pas grand chose
People tell me that our lives aren't worth much

Elles passent en un instant comme fanent les roses
They go by in an instant like fading roses.

On me dit que le temps qui glisse est un salaud
People tell me that the time which slips by is a bastard

Que de nos tristesses il s'en fait des manteaux
Who clothes himself in our sorrows

Pourtant quelqu'un m'a dit...
And yet someone told me...

Que tu m'aimais encore, c'est quelqu'un qui m'a dit...
That you still loved me, did they really tell me...

Que tu m'aimais encore, serait-ce possible alors?
That you still loved me, could it be possible?

Français
(in a nutshell)

Français Overview

For those of you who don't have the time for an in-depth study of the language… here are French basics in a nutshell:

Pro-nun-ci-ation

Listening to the radio or TV (in French of course) helps with the recognition of these sounds.

Silent letters

First a word on pronunciation. As you may know, in French there are a lot of letters which are not pronounced, especially those at the end of the word. Look at the words below:

ex. **le chat (luh sha)**- the cat
ex. **les chats (lay sha)** - the cats

In the first example, the **"t"** on chat is not pronounced. In the plural form, both the **"t"** and the **"s"** are silent. So, there is no difference in pronunciation between the singular and plural form of the word cat. The difference is in the article **"le"** (luh) vs. **"les"** (lay)

il chante (he sings)
ils chantent (they sing)
(**"ent"** at the end of a verb is silent)

In the "sing" example the **"ent"** of the plural verb is not pronounced. The result is that "he sings" and "they sing" sound exactly the same! The context of the situation is necessary to tell you which subject is intended.

Liaison

Another important aspect of French pronunciation is "liaison" or linking. Liaison occurs when a normally silent letter is pronounced because the word following it begins with a vowel. The example below shows liaison in action:

"Ils ont"- they have
The **"s"** is pronounced as a **"z"** sound
like **"il-zont"**

Pro-nun-ci-ation

A note about the French **"R"**. The French R is guttural, meaning that the sound is produced, not on the tongue as in Spanish or Italian, but from the throat. Practice clearing your throat– **that's the French R!**

Pratice: **Robert (roh-bear)**
Paris (pah-ree)
rat (rah)- rat
pourquoi (por-kwah)- why

The French Accents

French accents are an important part of spelling and pronunciation. In French there are **5 different accents:**

accent aigu: **J'ai mangé** (I ate).
This accent gives the ending of the verb the **"ay"** sound.

accent grave: **mon père** (my father).
This accent gives the **"e"** a shorter, clipped sound.

accent cedille: **français** (French).
This accent softens the c to an **"s"** sound

accent circonflexe: **hôpital** (hospital).
This accent is a vestige of an **"s"** in older French which used to follow the vowel.

accent tréma: **Noël** (Christmas).
This accents indicates that the two vowels are pronounced separately.

Pah-ree
lay-sha

Articles & Gender

In French, as in Spanish and Italian, nouns are either masculine or feminine. There is no set pattern for determining the gender of a noun based on the nature of the word or its ending. Some words like "man" or "woman" are inherently masculine or feminine, but other words like "paper", "pen" or "apple" have no inherent gender. As you acquire vocabulary, pay attention to the word's gender by learning the article along with the word.

The definite articles which accompany nouns are the following:

le- the (masculine, singular)
la- the (feminine, singular)
l'- the (masculine and feminine singular before a word beginning with a vowel
les- the (masculine and feminine plural).
Look at the following examples:

feminine	masculine
la table (the table)	**le stylo** (the pen)
la chanson (the song)	**le livre** (the book)
l'école (the school)	**l'animal** (the animal)

Pay attention to the word's gender by learning the article along with the word.

The indefinite articles are as follows:

un- a, an, one (masculine singular)
une- a, an, one (feminine singular)
des- some* (masculine and feminine plural)

*(in English **"des"** is often not translated into anything)

une femme (a woman)	**un homme** (a man)
une chanteuse (a singer)	**un chanteur** (a singer)
des filles ((some) girls)	**des garçons** ((some) boys)

Pronouns & Conjugations

In French there are **9 subject pronouns**. They are:

Je- I	**Nous**- we
Tu- you (informal, singular)	**Vous- you** (singular formal, plural formal/informal)
Il- he	**Ils**- they (masculine)
Elle- she	**Elles**- they (feminine)
On- one	

As you can see, gender and number are important considerations when choosing the correct subject pronoun. Another important factor is the level of "formality" you wish to convey when communicating. In French you would use **"tu"** with family and friends. Generally, you would use **"vous"** with an adult you do not know well. It is always better to start of being formal with someone if you are not sure whether to use the **"tu"** or **"vous"**. If the person is OK with **"tu"** they will tell you to address them with **"tu"**.

Once you have decided on which subject pronoun to use, you'll need to "conjugate your verb", matching it up with the subject pronoun. In French there are regular patterns for the verbs which make it easy for you to know how to conjugate. Here are the three main groups of verbs with their patterns.

Pronouns & Conjugations

"ER" verbs	"IR" verbs*	"RE" verbs
parler (to speak)	**dormir** (to sleep)	**vendre** (to sell)
je parle	**je dors**	**je vends**
tu parles	**tu dors**	**tu vends**
il parle	**il dort**	**il vend**
elle parle	**elle dort**	**elle vend**
on parle	**on dort**	**on vend**
nous parlons	**nous dormons**	**nous vendons**
vous parlez	**vous dormez**	**vous vendez**
ils parlent	**ils dorment**	**ils vendent**
téléphoner (to phone)	**courir (to run)**	**attendre (to wait for)**
chanter (to sing)	**dormir (to sleep)**	**boire (to drink)**
visiter (to visit)	**partir (to leave)**	**dire (to say)**
voyager (to travel)	**venir (to come)**	**prendre (to take)**

*There is a second category of **"IR"** verbs which add an extra syllable **"iss"** in the plural verb forms:

Finir (to finish)

je **finis**
tu **finis**
il **finit**
elle **finit**
on **finit**
nous **finissons**
vous **finissez**
ils **finissent**
elles **finissent**

Verbs conjugated like **finir** are:

choisir (to choose)
réussir (to succeed)
grandir (to grow)
grossir (to gain wieght)
maigrir (to lose weight)
vieillir (to grow older)

Irregular Verbs

There are several irregular verbs in French where there is no set pattern, so you'll have to memorize these forms. The four cornerstones of French verbs (verbs crucial for forming the past and future tenses, and verbs used in a number of idiomatic expressions), happen to be irregular. They are:

j'ai	**je suis**	**je fais**	**je vais**
tu as	**tu es**	**tu fais**	**tu vas**
il a	**il est**	**il fait**	**il va**
elle a	**elle est**	**elle fait**	**elle va**
on a	**on est**	**on fait**	**on va**
nous avons	**nous sommes**	**nous faisons**	**nous allons**
vous avez	**vous êtes**	**vous faites**	**vous allez**
ils ont	**ils sont**	**ils font**	**ils vont**
elles ont	**elles sont**	**elles font**	**elles vont**

Here are a few idiomatic expressions with **"avoir"** and **"faire"**.

avoir:

J'ai froid. (I'm cold.)
Vous avez soif? (You're thirsty?)
Ils ont faim. (They are hungry.)
Elle a 35 ans. (She is 35 years old.)
Ils ont de la chance. (They are lucky.)
Il a peur du chien. (He is afraid of the dog.)
Nous avons besoin de partir. (We need to leave.)

Note: In English we use the verb **"to be"** for these expressions.

faire:

Il fait beau. (The weather is nice.)
Il fait mauvais. (The weather is bad.)
Je fais la cuisine. (I'm cooking/ I cook.)
Elle fait ses valises. (She is packing her suitcases.)
Nous faisons attention. (We pay attention.)

To "Know" & to make a "No"

To "Know" in French

In French there are two verbs to express knowing.
You would use **"savoir"** in cases where you know information or facts.
You would use **"connaître"** in cases where you are familiar with a place, a thing or a person.

Savoir	**Connaître**
je sais	**je connais**
tu sais	**tu connais**
il sait	**il connaît**
elle sait	**elle connaît**
on sait	**on connaît**
nous savons	**nous connaissons**
vous savez	**vous connaissez**
ils savent	**ils connaissent**

Il ne sait pas mon numéro de téléphone. (He doesn't know my phone number.)
Est-ce que tu sais nager? (Do you know how to swim?)
Je ne sais pas pourquoi il aime ce film (I don't know why he likes this film.)

Je ne connais pas Jean-Marc. (I don't know Jean-Marc.)
Tu connais ce restaurant? (Do you know this restaurant?)
Il connaît très bien la France (He knows France very well.)

Negating Your Sentences

To form negatives in French you place a **"ne"** before the verb and a **"pas"** immediately after the verb. Here are some example

J'ai un vélo (I have a bicycle)
Je n'ai pas de voiture (I don't have a car)
(Note: **ne** changes to **n'** before a vowel)

Je suis français (I am French)
Je ne suis pas américain. (I am not American)

Nous parlons français. (We speak French.)
Nous ne parlons pas japonais (We don't speak Japanese.)

Questions?

There are three ways to form a question in French:

The simplest way is to use intonation, raising your voice slightly at the end of the question.

The second way is to add **"Est-ce que"**(eska) to the beginning of your sentence.

The third way is to invert your subject with your verb and put a hyphen between the two. This is called "inversion".

Check out these examples:
1. (with intonation) **Tu es français?** (You're French?)
2. **Est-ce que tu es français?** (Are you French?)
3. **Es-tu français** (Are you French?)

For more complex questions you would simply put the desired "question word" at the beginning of the sentence. The answer you receive will give you information above and beyond a simple "yes or no". Here are some common question words:

Pourquoi (why)
Où (where)
Avec qui (with whom)
Quand (when)
Qui (who/whom)
Comment (how)

Here are a couple of examples using various question structures and question words:

Pourquoi est-ce que tu aimes le français?
(Why do you like French?)
Parce que c'est très beau!
(Because it's very beautiful.)
Quand vont-ils à la plage?
(When are they going to the beach?)
Ils vont à la plage à 11 heures du matin.
(They are going to the beach at 11:00AM.)
Qui est dans la cuisine?
(Who is in the kitchen?)
Pierre est dans la cuisine.
(Pierre is in the kitchen.)

Useful Expressions

The Essentials

oui (yes)
non (non)
merci (thank you)
merci beaucoup (thank you very much)
où sont les toilettes? (Where is the bathroom?)
aidez-moi! (help me!)
parlez plus lentement s'il vous plaît (speak slower please
combien coûte ... ? (How much is...)

Greetings

Bonjour! (Hello)
Salut (Hi, informal)
Bonsoir (Good evening)
Bonne nuit (Good night)
Au revoir (Good-bye)
A bientôt (See you soon)
A tout à l'heure (See you in a bit)
C'est un plaisir de faire votre connaissance.
(It's a pleasure to meet you.)
Enchanté(e) (Nice to meet you.)
Comment vous appelez-vous?
(What is your name?- formal)
Comment t'appelles-tu? (What is your name?- informal)
Je m'appelle.... (My name is...)
D'où êtes-vous? (Where are you from? - formal)
D'où es-tu? (Where are you from?- informal)
Je suis de... (I'm from...)
Quel âge avez-vous? (How old are you? - formal)
Quel âge as-tu? (How old are you? - informal)
J'ai ... ans. (I am ... years old.)
Parlez-vous anglais? (Do you speak English?)
Non, je parle français seulement. (No I only speak French.)
Excusez-moi, Je ne parle pas bien le français.
(Excuse me, I don't speak French well.)

Salut!

Useful Expressions

Directions

Excusez-moi, pour aller à .... s'il vous plaît?
(Excuse me, how do I get to... please?)
Où se trouve ....? (Where is...?)
C'est à combien de kilomètres d'ici?
(How many kilometers is it from here?)
Où est la station-service la plus proche s'il vous plaît?
(Where is the nearest gas station please?)

à gauche **(left)**

à droite **(right)**

tout droit **(straight ahead)**

devant **(in front of)**

derrière **(in back of)**

à côté de **(next to)**

en face de **(across from)**

ici **(here)**

there **(là-bas, là)**

près **(near, close)**

loin **(far)**

vers **(toward)**

la rue **(the street)**

le carrefour **(intersection)**

Numbers

0. **zéro**
1. **un**
2. **deux**
3. **trois**
4. **quatre**
5. **cinq**
6. **six**
7. **sept**
8. **huit**
9. **neuf**
10. **dix**
12. **douze**
13. **treize**
14. **quatorze**
15. **quinze**
16. **seize**
17. **dix-sept**
18. **dix-huit**
19. **dix-neuf**
20. **vingt**
21. **vingt et un**
22. **vingt-deux**

30. **trente**
40. **quarante**
50. **cinquante**
60. **soixante**
70. **soixante-dix**
80. **quatre-vingts**
90. **quatre-vingt-dix**
100. **cent**
101. **cent un**
200. **deux cents**
1000. **mille**
2000. **deux mille**
100,000. **cent mille**
1,000,000. **un million**

When ranking things in order use:

premier / première (first)
deuxième (second)
troisième (third)
quatrième (fourth)
cinquième (fifth)
sixième (sixth)
septième (seventh)
huitième (eighth)
neuvième (ninth)
dixième (tenth)

Time & Days

Avez-vous l'heure s'il vous plaît?
(Do you have the time please)

Quelle heure est-il? (What time is it?)

Il est... (It's...)
une heure (one o'clock)
une heure et demie (one thirty)
deux heures (two o'clock)
deux heures et quart (two fifteen)
trois heures moins dix (ten minutes to three)
trois heures moins le quart (a quarter to three)
neuf heures du soir (nine p.m.)
neuf heures du matin (nine a.m.)
midi (noon)
minuit (midnight)

Quel jour sommes-nous? (What day is it?)

Nous sommes ...
lundi (Monday)
mardi (Tuesday)
mercredi (Wednesday)
jeudi (Thursday)
vendredi (Friday)
samedi (Saturday)
dimanche (Sunday)

demain, c'est... (Tomorrow is...)

aujourd'hui, c'est (Today is...)

hier était... (Yesterday was...)

Glossary

(m.) denotes a masculine noun
(f.) denotes a feminine noun

A

a (avoir)- he/she/it has
à- to, at, in, on, about
à côté de- next to
à moi- (of) my own
acheter (s'acheter)- to buy (to buy for each other)
achever (s'achever)- to end
agenda- day planner book (m.)
ai (avoir)- I have
ailes- wings (f.)
aimais (aimer)- I/you loved (imperfect form of the verb)
aimé- loved
aimer- to love, to like (**s'aimer**- to love each other); (**je t'aime**- I love you); (**il vous aime**- He loves you)
aimerais- I would like (similar to voudrais)
air- air (m.); (**avoir l'air de...**- to seem like...)
alentours- surroundings (m.)
allez (aller)- come on! (for encouragement)
alors- so, then
âme-soeur- soul mate (m.)
amis d'avant- friends from before (m.)
amour- love (m.)
ange- angel (m.)
anxiolytiques- anti-anxiety medications (f.)
apparaître- to appear
appel- the calling, the call (m.)
applaudisse (applaudir)- to applaud (subjunctive form)
apprendre- to learn
arc-en-ciel- rainbow (m.)
archange- archangel (m.)
armes- arms, weapons (f). (sans armes- unarmed)
arracher- tear off, tear out
Atlantique- the Atlantic ocean (m.)
attacher- to attach
attends (attendre)- I/you wait (for); (**attendais**- I was waiting -imperfect form)
au mépris du- regardless
aube- the dawn (f.)
aucun- not a single, no (adjective)
aujourd'hui- today
autour- around
autre- another
avais (j'avais, from avoir)- I had
avait (avoir)- he/she/it had (**il nous avait changé**- it had changed us)
avec- with
aventurière- adventurous (feminine form o the adjective)
avenue- avenue (f.)
avoir- to have

B

baigne (baigner)- to bathe
beau- beautiful (masculine form of the adjective)
beaucoup- a lot
belle- beautiful (feminine form of the adjec tive)
besoin- need (m.); (**avoir besoin de...**- to need...)
bête- silly, stupid
bien- well (adverb); (**quelqu'un de bien**- someone good)
bien mort- really dead
(en) bikini- in a bikini
blancs/blanches- white (plural adjective, m. / f.)
blessés- wounded (masculine, plural adjective)
bohème- bohemian
boire- to drink
bonheur- happiness (m.)
bonjour- hello
booké- booked
bottes- boots (f)
bouddhiste- Buddhist
bouger- to move
boule- ball (f.)
boulevards- boulevards (m.)
bout- the end (m.); (**le bout du monde**- the end (furthest reaches) of the earth); (**à bout de**- at the end of)
bras-arm(s) (m.)
brille (briller)- to shine
brűle (brűler)- to burn

C

ça- it, that (demonstrative pronoun)
ça et là- here and there

Glossary

café crème- espresso with milk
cantatrice- singer (f.)
ce (c')- this (demonstrative adjective); (**c'est tout**- that's it)
ce- it (pronoun)
ce que- what (relative pronoun)
celle- the one (feminine form)
cendres- ashes (f.)
certitude- certainty (f.)
cet- this (masculine demonstrative adjective); (**cet amour**- this love)
cette- this (feminine demonstrative adjective)
chacun- each person
chagrin(s)- sorrow(s) (m.); (**peau de chagrin**- literally, skin of sorrow or shagreen)
chambre- the bedroom (f.)
changé (changer)- changed
chanter- to sing
chaque- each
chavirer- to reel
chemin- way, path (m.)
cher- dear (adjective)
cheri- darling (m.)
cherche (chercher)- to look for
Chiapas- a state in southeast Mexico.
chienne- a female dog, (bitch); (**vie de chienne**- a wretched life)
chinois- chinese (m.)
chose- thing (f.)
ciel- heaven, sky (m.)
cinéma- movie; (**faire du cinéma**- to make movies)
claques- slaps (f.)
claquettes- tapdancing (f. pl.); (**faire des claquettes**- to tap dance)
clash- clash (m.)
classe- class, style (f.)
clic-clac- sofa bed (m.)
coeur(s)- heart(s) (m.)
coin- the corner (m.)
coincer- to wedge
comme- how, like, as, (**comme si**- as if)
complémentaire- complementary
compléter- to complete
compte (compter)- to count
conditionnel- the conditional form of the verb (m.)
consonne(s)- consonant(s) (f.)
conversation- conversation (f.)
cour- courtyard, playground (f.)
cours (courir)- to run
crever (se crever)- break, (**j'en crève**- I'm dying from it)
crois (croire)- I/you think
croiser (se croiser)- to cross paths, to meet up
crus- harsh (masculine, plural form of the adjective)

D

dans- in
dansez (danser)- to dance
de (d')- of, from
décombres- the rubble
découvrir- to discover
délices- delights (f.)
demain- tomorrow (m.)
dents- teeth (f.); (**laisser des dents**- to endure hardship, to literally lose one's teeth)
déployées- unfurled
depuis (que)- since
des- some (indefinite article, plural)
dès qu'il- as soon as
désert- desert (m.)
déserté (déserter)- to desert, abandon
désirer- to desire
désormais- from now/then on
dessiner- to draw
destin- destiny (m.)
déteste (détester)- to hate
détours- detours (**sans détours**- direct)
deux- two (m.)
devant- in front of
devenir- to become (**je deviendrais**- I would/might become...); (**deviennent**- they become)
diable- devil (m.)
dire- to say
dis (dire)- tell (dis-moi-tell me)
dit (dire)- he/she tells (also the past participle of the verb **dire**); (**on me dit que...**- people tell me that...); (**on m'a dit que...**- people told me that...)
dites (dire)- you tell
diva- diva (f.)
divine- divine (feminine form of the adjective)
donne (donner)- to give
doute- doubt (f.)
doux- mild
droit- upright, straight, right
du- of the (contraction of "de" and "le")
du- some (partitive article)

Glossary

dű (devoir)- (past participle of the verb devoir); (**J'ai dű**- I had to)

E

eau- water (f.)
éblouissait (éblouir)- to dazzle (imperfect form)
échoue (échouer)- to fail
école- school (f.)
écouter- to listen to
écrire- to write
édredon- the comforter (m.)
elles- they (feminine plural subject and disjunctive pronoun)
éloigne (éloigner)- to distance
émerveille (émerveiller)- amazes
emporte (emporter)- to carry away
en- in, of it (preposition or pronoun)
en plus- in addition
encore- still
en dehors de- outside of
ennui- boredom (m.)
ennuient (s'ennuyer)- to become bored
ennuies (ennuyer)- you annoy, bother, bore
enseigne (enseigner)- to teach
ensorcelle (ensorceller)- to captivate
entends (entendre)- I/you hear
entière- whole (feminine form of the adjective)
entre- between
entre-mêle (entre-mêler)- to interweave
épargné (épargner)- spared (past participle of the verb)
éradiquerait (éradiquer)- would eradicate
essaie (essayer)- tries
es (être)- (you) are
est (être)- (he/she/it) is
et- and
étais (être)- I used to be (imperfect form)
était (être)- he/she/it was (imperfect form)
été- summer (m.)
éternel- eternal
étincelle- spark (f.)
étrange- strange
étranger- unfamiliar (adjective)
être- to be
étoiles- the stars (f.)
évapore (s'evaporer)- to evaporate, to disappear
évite (éviter)- to avoid
extase- ecstacy (f.)

F

fait (faire)- it makes
faim- hunger (f.)
faire- to make (**ça le fait rire**- that makes him laugh); (**se faire**- to make (for) oneself)
faire l'amour- to make love
fanent (faner)- they fade
fantasme (fantasmer)- to fantasize
fasse- (subjunctive form of the verb **faire**)- to make
faubourgs- outskirts of a town (m.); (working class suburbs)
faut (falloir)- it is necessary (**il faut...**)
femme- woman (f.)
fenêtre- window (f.)
fidèle- faithful
figure- a figure (f.)
fille- girl (f.)
fin- the end (f.)
fini (finir)- ended (past participle of the verb); (**c'est fini**- it's over); (**tu as fini**- you finished (past tense)
finir- to finish
flamme- flame (f.)
flaques- puddles (f.)
flou- blurred
foi- faith (f.)
folle- crazy, mad (feminine form of adjective. The masculine form -fou); (**herbe folle**- wild grasses)
fontaines- fountains (f.)
force (à force de)- because of
fort- strong
fou- insane, crazy (feminine form of the adjective is folle)
foule- crowd, mob (f.)
foutu le camp- disappeared, took off
fringue- clothing (f.) (slang)
fuite- escape (f.); (**prendre la fuite**- to escape, run away)

G

garder- to keep
génie- genius (m.)
glisse (glisser)- to slide, slip
goűt de miel- honey flavored
grain- texture (m.)
grand (en grand)- wide
grave- solemn, serious
grisé (se griser)- to become drunk, intoxicated; (**je me suis grisé de**- I got drunk on)
grue- a crane, a call-girl (slang) (f.)

guérilla- geurilla fighter; (**faire la guérilla**- to be a guerilla fighter)
guerrière- a warrior (f.)
gueule- (faire la gueule)- to become silent, sulk

H

hanches- hips (f.)
herbe- grass (f.)
hermite (en hermite)- as a hermit
heures- hours (f.)
histoire- story (f.)
huit- eight (m.)

I

idoles- idols (f.)
il- he, it (subject pronoun)
il y a- there is, there are, ago
Ille-et-Vilaine- a department in Brittany, France
implore (implorer)- to implore, beg
importe (importer)- he/she/it matters
importent (importer)- they matter
indépendant- independent
inquiétude- anxiety (f.)
instant- an instant (m.)
invente (inventer)- to invent

J

jazz- jazz (m.)
je- I (subject pronoun)
jetez (jeter)- you throw
jour- day (m.)
journée- day (f.)
juste- just

K

L

là- there
la- the (feminine definite article)
lac(s)- lake(s) (m.)
laisse-moi- let me (go), allow me
laisser- to leave
lamentablement- miserably
le- the, it, him (definite article, direct object pronoun) (m.)
léger- light (adjective)
lendemain- the next day (m.)
les- the, them (definite article, direct object) (plural)
lettre- letter (f.)
lit- bed (m.)
livre- book (m.)
lourd- heavy
lui- (to) him (indirect object and disjunctive pronoun)

M

ma- my (feminine form of the possessive adjective)
main(s)- hand(s) (f.)
maintenant- now
mais- but
mal- harm (m.)
malice- mischief, harm (f.)
manque (manquer)- to be missing
manteau(x)- coat(s) (m.); (**il s'en fait des manteaux**- literally, he makes coats out of, he clothes himself in...)
marchais (marcher)- I used to walk, I was walking (imperfect tense)
(en) marchant- by walking
marcherai (marcher)- I will walk
mature- mature
me (m')- me (direct and indirect object pronoun)
méditer- to meditate
méfier (se méfier de)- to be wary of
meilleure- better (feminine form of the adjective)
mêle (se mêler)- blend
même- even, same (**en même temps**- at the same time)
même plus- not any more
mène (mener)- to lead
mes- my (plural form)
mine de rien- casually, without being obvious
miroir- the mirror (m.)
moi- me (emphatic pronoun, disjunctive pronoun)
moi-même- myself
moins- less
mon- my (masculine form)
mondaine- to be a socialite (feminine form of the adjective)
monde- the world (m.)
montgolfière- hot air balloon (f.)
moque (se moquer)- to mock
morceau(x)- piece(s) (m.)
mort- dead (adjective)
mots- words (m.)
murmure (murmurer)- to murmur

Glossary

N

ne (n')... pas- not (structure used to negate verbs)
ne (n')... plus- no longer (structure used to negate verbs)
ne (n')... rien- nothing
neuf- nine
nez- nose (m.)
noir(e)- dark, black
nombre- number (m.)
non plus- neither
nord- the north (m.)
nos- our (possessive adjective, plural object)
note(s)- note(s) (f.)
notre- our (possessive adjective, singular object)
nous- us, we (subject pronoun, direct/ indirect object pronoun, disjunctive pronoun)
nous-même- ourselves
nouveau- new (masculine form of the adjective)
nuit(s)- night(s) (f.)
numéro- number (m.)

O

ô combien- oh how much (exclamatory)!
on- one, people or we (general use), (subject pronoun)
opéra- the opera (m.)
ordinaire- ordinary
oreille- ear (f.); (**à mon oreille**- to myself)
ou- or
oů- where
oublie (oublier)- to forget
oui- yes
ouvre (s'ouvrir)- to open up

P

paire- pair (f.)
par- by
paraît (paraître)- it seems
parce que- because
parfois- sometimes
parfume (se parfumer à...)- to perfume oneself with...
parle (parler)- I speak, he/she speaks
parole(s)- words (f.)
part en sucette- to fall apart, degenerate
pas- footstep (m.) au pas- in the footsteps
pas (ne...pas)- structure used to negate verbs
pas plus- no more
passant- passer-by (m.)
passe (passer)- to pass
peau- skin (f.)
peintre- painter (m.)
penche (se pencher)- to lean over
pense (penser)- I think, he/she thinks (**penses**- you think)
perdu (perdre)- lost (past participle of the verb)
petit- little
peu- little (**un peu- a little**); (**peu de temps**- a short while)
peut (pouvoir)- he/she/one can
peut-être- maybe
peux (pouvoir)- I/you can
pièce(s)- piece(s) (f.)
pied(s)- foot (feet) (m.)
pilote de l'air- airplane pilot (m.)
planète- planet (f.)
pluie- rain (f.)
plume(s)- feather(s) (f.)
plus- (the) more
plus (ne...plus)- no more, no longer
pointé (se pointer)- to appear, come into being
portée- reach (f.); (**à portée de main**- within arm's (hand's) reach)
portent (porter)- they carry
portes- doors (f.)
pour- for
pour que- so that (this conjunction is followed by a verb in the subjunctive mode)
pourquoi- why
pourrais (from the verb pouvoir)- I could (conditional form)
poursuit (poursuivre)- he/she/one pursues
pourtant- yet, still
préfère (préférer)- I/he/she/one prefer(s)
prélude- prelude (m.)
premier- first
prends (prendre)- I/you take
prénom- first name (m.)
près de- near
présent(e)- present (**à présent**- now)
profond- deep
profondeur(s)- depth(s) (f.)
promesse(s)- promise(s) (f.)
promet (promettre)- to promise
puis- then

Glossary

puis (pouvoir alternate form)- I can (**je ne puis plus...**- I can no longer...)

Q

quand- when
quand même- all the same, even so
quatre- four
que- that, may (may the devil carry me away); so that (so that I may make my own movie)
quelqu'un- someone
qu'est-ce que c'est- what is it?
qu'est-ce que c'est bon- how nice it is
qui- which, that (relative pronoun)
qui est-ce qui- who
quincher- to dance
quitte (quitter)- to leave

R

raconte (raconter)- to tell (a story)
recoller- to glue back together
recolter- to harvest
rapporteur- informant (m.)
redoublé (redoubler)- intensified
regard- a look, the eyes (m)
regarde (regarder)- look
relâche- pause, break, rest (f.); (**sans relâche**- relentlessly)
remous- turmoil (m.)
remplit (remplir)- to fill
renseigne (renseigner)- to inform, give information
(se) renseigner- to figure things out, to become informed
renverser- to turn upside down
répare (réparer)- to repair
repeter (se repeter)- to repeat
reporter- reporter (m.)
résister- to resist
reste (rester)- to stay, remain (on restera- one will remain (future tense))
reste- the rest (m.)
retiendra (retenir)- will hold back (future form)
retire (retirer)- to remove
retomber- to fall back down
retrouvé (retrouver)- to find again (**Je t'ai retrouvé**- I found you again); (**on se retrouve**- one finds oneself)
rêve- to dream (m.)
réveil (m.)- moment when one wakes up
rêver- to dream
reviens (revenir)- come back
revolte (revolter)- to appal
révolutionnaire- revolutionary
rien (ne... rien)- nothing
rien de plus- nothing more
rien d'autre- nothing else
rire- to laugh
rocher- rock (m.)
roller- rollerblading (m.); (**faire du roller**- to go rollerblading)
roses- roses (f.)
rue(s)- street(s) (f.)

S

sa- his, her (feminine form)
sage- sage, wise man (m.)
salaud- bastard (m.)
salon- the sitting room (m.)
samedi- Saturday (**les samedis**- on Saturdays)
sang- blood (m.)
sans- without
sais (savoir)- I/you know
secret- secret (feminine form of the adjective is **secrète**)
semer- to sow
sens- sense(s) (m.)
serait (être)- would (conditional form of the verb **être**); (**serait-ce possible?** literally, Would it be possible?)
serbe- Serbian (m.)
seul- alone (masculine form of the adjective, "**seule**" is the feminine form)
seulement- only
si- so, if (**si doux**- so mild)
soirées- parties (f.)
soleil- sun (m.)
solitaire- alone
sombre (sombrer)- to sink, to get sad
sommeil- sleep (m.)
son- his/her (masculine form)
sonde (sonder)- I probe
sont (être)- they are
sors (sortir)- I exit (**je sors du lit**- I get out of bed)
sort- fate
souffrir- to suffer
soufflé (souffler)- blew (past participle of the verb)
sous- under
souviens (se souvenir)- to remember (**Je ne me souviens plus**- I don't remember anymore)

star- star (f.)
succès- success (m.)
suis (ètre)- (I) am; **suis-je**- am I? (inversion structure is used with questions)
sur- on

T

tant- so much
tard- late
te (t')- you (direct/indirect object pronoun)
temps- weather (m.)
temps- time (m.) (in certain expression); (**il est grand temps**- it's about time)
tend (tendre)- he/she/one reaches out
tête- head (f.)
toi- you (disjunctive and emphatic pronoun)
tomber- to fall, drop (**laisser tomber**- to drop the subject)
ton- your (possessive adjective)
toujours- forever, always, still
tour- turn, trip (m.); (**faire le tour du monde**- take a trip around the world)
tourner- to turn
tout- everything (also the adjective "all" in the masculine form)
toutes- all (adjective in the feminine form)
tout d'un coup- all of a sudden
tout ce qui- all that is
trait(s)- the features (of a face) (m.)
très- very
triste- sad
traverser- to cross
tréma- diaeresis accent (m.)
tristesse(s)- sadness(es) (f.)
trois- three
trop (de trop, trop de)- too much
trottoirs- sidewalks (m.)
troublé (se troubler)- become blurry
trouvé (trouver)- found
trouverais (trouver)- I would find (the conditional form of the verb)
tu- you (subject pronoun)

U

un- a, an, one (m.) (indefinite article, number)
une- a, an (f.) (indefinite article)

V

va (aller)- it/he/she goes
vaccin- vaccine (m.)
vais (aller)- I go, I'm going (used to form a future tense when combined with infinitive verbs)
valent (valoir)- they are worth
velours- velvet (m.)
vent(s)- wind(s) (m.)
vers- towards
veux (vouloir)- I want
vies- lives (f.)
viens (venir)- come (imperative form of th verb)
vilain- ugly, to be an eyesore
vingt ans- 20 years
vive (vivre) le un- long live the one (exclamatory, verb is in the subjunctive mood)
vivre- to live
voilà- that's it, here it is
voilés- veiled (masculine plural form of the adjective)
voilier- sailboat (m.)
vois (voir)- I/you see
voix- voice (f.)
voler- to fly
voudrais (vouloir)- I/you would like (conditional form, polite)
voudrait (vouloir)- he/she/one would like (conditional form, polite)
vous- you (subject pronoun, direct/indirect object pronoun, disjunctive pronoun)
voyelle(s)- vowel(s) (f.)
vrai- true
vraiment- really, truly
vu (voir)- seen, given (past participle of the verb)
vulnérable- vulnerable

W

X

Y

y- there (pronoun replacing places)
y a que- there is only (shortened from: **il n'y a que**)
yeux- eyes (m,pl.) singular- **un oeil** (**les yeux dans les yeux**- gazing into each others eyes)
yoga- yoga (m.); (**faire du yoga**- to do yoga)

Z

Notes

Notes

Notes

Credits

AMELIA "ET VOUS"
Written and performed by Amelia
From album «After All» (Jesse Emerson/ Teisha Helgerson/ Scott Weddle)
Published 2004
Courtesy of Slow Down Records

CARLA BRUNI "RAPHAEL"
Performed by Carla Bruni
Written and composed by Carla Bruni
(p) & © 2002 naïve
With courtesy of naïve

ISRC: FR 47Q 02 00560

CARLA BRUNI "QUELQU'UN M'A DIT"
Composed and performed by Carla Bruni
Written by Carla Bruni and Leos Carax
(p) & © 2002 naïve
With courtesy of naïve

ISRC: FR 47Q 02 00550

CORALIE CLEMENT "C'EST LA VIE"
Written by Benjamin Biolay
Published 2009 by Bambi Rose
Performed by Coralie Clement
From album «Toystore»
Courtesy of Compass Music & Discograph Records
Licensed with Discograph, France (world)
Licensed with Compass Records, USA (N. America)

EMILIE SIMON "DESERT"
Written and performed by Emilie Simon
From album «Emilie Simon»
Published 2003 by Vegetal
Courtesy of Milan Entertainment & Vegetal Publishing
Licensed with Milan Entertainment, USA

FRANCOIZ BREUT "LA CERLITUDE"
Written by Jerome Miniere
Performed by Francoiz Breut
From album «Une Saison Volee»
Published 2006
Courtesy of PIK
Licensed with OPIK Music, France

HOUSE DE RACKET "1,2,3,4"
(Pierre Leroux, Victor le Masne)
Performed by Housse De Racket
From album «Forty Love»
(P) & © 2008 M2o Solutions/ Kuskus under licence to Discograph (France, Belgium, Switzerland)
With kind permission of M2o Solutions/ Kuskus/ Discograph

JEAN RACINE "ENTRE NOUS"
Written and performed Jean Racine
From album «Ivre Du Son»
Published 2007
Courtesy of Delabel
Licensed with Roy Music Group, France

MADEMOISELLE K "FRINGUE PAR FRINGUE"
Written and performed by Katerine Gierak and Mademoiselle K
From album «Ca Me Vexe»
Published 2006
Courtesy of Roy Music
Licensed with Roy Music Group, France

MARIANNE FEDER "JE VAIS PEUT-ETRE ATTENDRE DENAIN"
Written and performed by Marianne Feder
From album «Toi Mon Indien»
Published 2008
Courtesy of Lepic et Colegram
Licensed with Lepic et Colegram, France

MELANIE PAIN "CELLE DE MES 20 ANS"
Written by Pap Deziel/ Villeneuve
Published 2009
Performed by Melanie Pain from album «My Name»
Courtesy of Kwaida Records

OLIVER LIBAUX AND BARBARA "CELLE DE MES 20 ANS"
Written by Oliver Libaux
Published 2009
Performed by Oliver Libaux feat Barbara Carlotti from album «Imbecile»
Courtesy of Discograph Records

PINK MARTINI "O ESTE MA TETE"
Music and lyrics by Alex Marashian, China Forbes and Thomas M. Lauderdale
From album «Splendor in the Grass»
Published by Alex Marashian Music (ASCAP), Wow & Dazzle Music (BMI) and Thomas M. Lauderdale Music (ASCAP)

Special "Thanks" to:

Graphic Design: Kate Wojtan; www.magicmustache.com

French Translations, French Basics and Glossary complied by Steve Stella – Graduate from UCLA and currently French professor at Windward School in Los Angeles, CA.